STAND FIRM

The Teenager's Guide to Self-Defense

MICHAEL JAMES

D0907684

SCHOLASTIC BOOK SERVICES
New York Toronto London Auckland Sydney Tokyo

for
Michael and James

ISBN 0-590-30033-4

12 11 10 9 8 7 6 5 4 3 2   3 4 5 6 7 8/8

TABLE OF CONTENTS

INTRODUCTION

When was the last time you picked a fight? Chances are that your answer will be "Never." The simple fact is most of us don't like to fight. And if all of us were like most of us, a book like this would never have to be written. Unfortunately, however, there are people who like to make trouble, and it is someone like yourself who ends up getting hurt. There isn't one of us who doesn't face the danger of being attacked.

Every school and every neighborhood has kids who get their kicks from hurting those who are weaker than themselves. In one small New Jersey community, an eighth grader paid $1,680 in daily "protection" payments during the first few months of a school year. Thirteen boys were involved in the shakedown. Frightened of getting beaten up, the victim paid for his safety by stealing the money from his parents .

If only this boy had had the ability to resist! That's what this book is all about. There come times in each of our lives when we have to stand up and fight back. There's simply no other way. This book will teach you how to do it.

You will not be taught how to kill or how to cripple for the fun of it. You won't learn any secrets that will make you "king of the hill." Rather, you will be taught how to develop a sense of strength and pride by knowing how to stand your ground when it is necessary to do so.

How To Read This Book

This book is different from those that you have read before. You'll get more from it if you use it with a friend, instead of reading it alone. Here's why: Self-defense can't be learned just by reading words and looking at pictures. Like boxing or dancing, you can't go too far without a partner.

If you really want to use this book properly and learn something, make it come to life. Each time you come to an explanation, you and your partner should stop and practice the motions that are being described and pictured. Take the time to get it right.

Every defense pattern involves a *predator* and a *victim*. Take turns with your friend at playing each role. First you be the bad guy, and let your friend take the defense. Try that until your friend stops you every time. Then reverse the parts and see how well you survive as the victim. Remember that each strategy must be practiced over and over until it becomes instinctive. In a moment of crisis you don't have time to plan your moves, you just have to react and move fast.

All the pictures in the book, by the way, are posed and not scenes of actual conflict. This is the best way of getting clear illustrations of the strategies being described. Note also that all instructions are based on the assumption that you are right-handed. If you are a lefty, it won't make a difference in most cases. From time to time, however, you might have to work out an adjustment.

Here's a bit of advice. Don't be *too* serious. Try to enjoy yourself. You and your partner will probably enjoy a good laugh every now and then. At the same time, don't lose sight of the importance of your goals — pride and confidence.

And if there are any girls out there who pick up this book, please don't put it down. This book was written with you in mind too. And it might just save your life. What girls might lack in brawn, they make up for in swiftness and agility. Today girls are taking combat training in all branches of the armed forces, as well as at the military academies, and they are earning the respect of their comrades. Pity the mugger who picks on a Marine, whether the Marine is male or female.

Caution!

As a final recommendation, be *very careful* using this book. You could easily get hurt, and this you don't need. Normally you don't even want to hurt others when they pick on you. You just want to let them know that you're not an easy mark.

Never strike an actual blow during practice. Learn to pull your punches. Save your strength for an old mattress or pillows. If a routine involves hitting the ground, work only on mats, sand, or soft turf. In short, let common sense be the rule.

But now it's time for you to get to work. Good luck!

·1·
WHO WANTS
TO FIGHT?

The first rule of self-defense is to avoid a fight whenever you can. Unfortunately, this isn't always easy to do. Some characters seem to enjoy making trouble, and keeping away from them is often impossible. It will help you to stay out of trouble, however, if you understand a few of the reasons that make a person pick a fight.

In every branch of the animal kingdom, from the ant to the hippo, peace depends largely on *territoriality*. The lion, for example, stakes out a claim over a clearly defined territory. Within the boundaries of this region he and his pride live a tranquil life. Only if another male tries to invade his domain will he fight.

Nations behave in much the same way. Peace is best preserved by not trespassing.

If you think about it, you'll realize that territoriality also exists in your neighborhood and in your school. Sometimes it's called "your own turf." You can get into hot water just by walking down the wrong street. By innocently sitting at a cafeteria table that is "claimed" you might be asking for a fight. There is neither logic nor legality to such claims, but nonetheless, there is no escaping the fact that they exist. And if you want to stay out of trouble, you often have to respect these claims.

Does this mean that you have to play the role of a coward, bowing to everyone else's will? Not at all. However, you should be aware of the hazards so you can plan in advance how to face them. Most often your best bet will be to shrug off claims that are of little consequence. Why have a fight just to sit at one table when another will do just as well? But, if your well-being is *seriously* threatened by an unfair claim, you must know how to take a stand.

Another thing that makes some people aggressive is their desire to maintain a position in their group. This is sometimes called pecking order, a term based on the behavior of barnyard chickens. Starting with the strongest, each chicken takes its turn at the food in a fixed order. A weaker bird who tries to get ahead of her place will quickly be pecked into submission by one who is stronger.

Isn't it pretty much the same at school and on the street? You can get along fine just as long as you don't step on someone's toes. The kids who do most of the fighting are the ones who are insecure about their rank. Learn to recognize these creeps and stay away from them.

Most schoolyard fights start for silly reasons. A good way to stay out of trouble, then, is to avoid doing anything that might threaten the status, real or imagined, of others. Individuals who feel threatened will attack by instinct. You will suffer no loss of dignity by walking around them every chance you get.

Have you ever seen a TV wildlife show about the life-style of gorillas? If so, you have seen another characteristic of animal aggression, the *ritualistic threat*. This is the mock battle that takes place between two individuals who are trying to determine superiority. Actual combat rarely takes place, because one of the contenders usually backs down under the other's frightening display of chest-thumping and shouts.

Have you ever seen the same thing at school? Bullies are experts at making noise. Most of them, however, are cowards at heart. Moreover, most of them perform only when they have members of their own group as an audience. *Never accept a challenge under such a circumstance.* If you do have to fight, make sure that you are in neutral territory. Once again, though, you should learn the art of looking the other way. Your mind must be as strong as your body. Know what issues are really important and those which are not.

To briefly sum up, you can stay out of most trouble by following three simple rules.

1. Don't invade somebody else's territory.
2. Don't threaten somebody else's rank.
3. Don't pay attention when somebody thumps his chest.

There are times, however, when you must stand up. If you allow yourself to be pushed around once, you will be fair game forever afterwards. You have to decide just how far you are willing to be pushed before pushing back. This decision can't be made at the moment you're being pushed. You must identify and affirm your values beforehand so that you will respond with confidence when that time arrives. In other words, you must be psychologically as well as physically prepared to defend yourself.

And here's something for you to think about. When you achieve the goal of self-reliance you will have an asset that goes far beyond the mere ability to defend yourself. You will be a new person, a person who is alive and vibrant. This is a reward which you can relish throughout your entire life.

·2·
KEEPING FIT

How did you feel when you woke up this morning? Did you leap out of bed, eager to face the day, or did you bury your head in the pillow and groan?

On your way to school was there a spring in your step, or did you drag your feet? Do you bounce or do you shuffle up a flight of stairs?

Sitting in class, is your mind alert to what is going on, or is your head outside doing something else?

The answers to all these questions are important. Unless you are fit both physically and mentally, no self-defense system will do you a bit of good.

Much information is available on the subject of fitness, and it is not within the scope of this book to outline a program for you. There are some basics, however, that might get you started, and you can take it from there.

First of all take a good, honest look at yourself. You probably have a lot going for you that you don't even know about. At the same time, like everyone else, you're not perfect.

Why don't you make a list of your strengths and a list of your weaknesses? Then ask yourself if you really take advantage of each strength, and what can you do to correct or offset each weakness. The zebra can't fight, for example, but it stays alive by outrunning the lion. The elephant can't run as fast, but when you're an elephant, who needs to run?

If you are tall, learn to use your reach effectively. If you are short, develop agility. If you are not muscular, learn the arts of balance and speed.

When was the last time that you had a physical examination? Perhaps there is some reason why you shouldn't play too rough. If you are overweight, maybe it's not just because of too many potato chips. If you are too thin, your doctor could recommend a diet.

What are your eating habits? The body of a teenager roars like a blast-furnace, and needs good and adequate fuel. A lot of kids do badly both in the classroom and in the gym because of poor nutrition. You should always eat a good breakfast, and when you go to the cafeteria for lunch, you should stay away from junk food.

How well you do throughout the day depends a lot on the way your day begins. Students of the Oriental arts place much importance on morning exercises, and you would do well to share their wisdom. In the following few pages a few simple warm-up exercises are described and pictured. Do them as soon as you get up in the morning, and see if you don't feel more alert throughout the day.

6

Four Points for Feeling Fit

1. Stand erect, hands on hips, and rotate your head and neck in as large a circle as you can. Do this several times in each direction (1a).

1a

2. Breathe in deeply while raising your arms in a long, taut stretch. Then, while exhaling slowly, bring your arms slowly back to your sides. Repeat this several times (1b).

1b

3. Place your hands on your hips, bend your knees slightly, and rotate your body in a wide, circular motion. Do this a few times, both clockwise and counter-clockwise (1c).

1c

4. Take an open stance, your arms extended sideward. Keeping your legs straight, bend to touch your left foot with your right hand. Return to position and then bend to touch your right foot with your left hand. Repeat this several times (1d).

1d

Remember that these are *warm-up* exercises, so take it easy. Their purpose will be defeated if you exhaust yourself doing them.

If you want to get into body-building exercises, you can find several instruction books in your school and local library. Here are a few simple exercises that you can use for starters. Each is designed to strengthen a particular part of your body.

Six Money-Saving Muscle-Builders

1. Wrist. Grasp an ordinary rubber ball in each hand and pump them in a tightening and relaxing rhythm. This can be done anytime you are out for a walk, or even when reading.

2. Arms and Chest. If you don't have weights, here's a neat trick. Grasp a towel as shown in the picture, pulling it as taut as you can throughout the exercise. Then, making believe that the towel is a barbell, go through the standard weight-lifting motions. The tension on your muscles caused by pulling on the towel will work your muscles as if you were using an actual barbell (2a).

2a

3. Shoulders. The well-known push-up is the best exercise. Be sure that only your hands and toes touch the floor. Start out by doing just a few, and then gradually increase the number (2b).

2b

4. Neck. Lace your fingers behind your neck and press your head back and forth against the pressure of your hands. You will feel your neck muscles being tested by the tension (2c).

2c

5. Stomach. Lie on your back, your hands laced behind your head. Keeping your legs stiff, alternately raise each as high as you can, and then slowly bring it back to position (2d).

2d

6. Legs. The familiar bicycle-ride exercise is good. So is the deep-knee bend. When doing knee bends, keep your torso straight as you go up and down (2e-2f).

2e

2f

There are probably millions of dollars worth of barbells rusting in basements throughout the country. Many kids make the mistake of spending a lot of money on weight-lifting equipment, only to abandon it when the novelty wears off.

You can save this money by using a little imagination. Arm exercises, for example, don't require fancy weights. A couple of ordinary bricks will do just as well. And you can substitute a regular bicycle tube for expensive springs used in arm exercises.

A Word For The Women...

Needless to say, a girl's physical fitness program should differ in many ways from that of a boy. Girls usually don't want bulging muscles. This doesn't mean, however, that their muscular network should be ignored. A reasonably athletic body makes a girl more attractive and feeling good. Exercise is important for everyone, regardless of sex.

Nothing conditions the body more enjoyably than active participation in sports. If you have any athletic ability at all, you should join teams at your school. Nobody says you have to be a big jock. Your physical-education instructors will help you in every way they can. But you have to go to them—they can't read your mind.

If your school doesn't already have them, you can help organize a jogging club, a hiking club, or a bicycle club. Remember, the service you get from your body in later life will depend largely on how well you get yourself put together now.

The message, then, is simple. You are as secure as you are fit. But fitness is more than just muscle. Fitness includes your body, your mind, and your emotions. If all of these are under control, you hopefully will never have to use a single defense instruction offered in this book. But if you ever need to, the next few chapters may be the most practical reading you'll ever do.

·3·
SELF-DEFENSE BY COMMON SENSE

You are out for a walk and up ahead you can see the way is blocked by a group of kids you don't know. Perhaps they won't bother you, but the possibility exists. What do you do? Do you square your shoulders and walk through them to prove that you are brave? If you do, you're out of your mind!

A large part of self-defense is common sense. Cross over and walk on the other side. If necessary do an about-face and choose a different route. There is no loss of self-respect in leaving a scene that smells like trouble. Almost every fight that takes place among teenagers could be avoided by the use of good judgment.

Have you noticed that some kids get picked on all the time, whereas others are left alone? This doesn't happen just by chance, and if you fall into the former category, there are ways that you can correct the situation.

A lot has to do with *body language*, a topic about which several books have been written. To put it in a nutshell, some people carry themselves in a way that invites attack. Certain mannerisms reveal weakness, and bullies like to prey on the weak.

Vulnerability is not a question of a person's size. You can be small and formidable, or you can be big and helpless. It's a question of your personal bearing. You get respect only if you *command* it.

Take a look at the boy in picture (3). His head is erect and his eyes are alert. His shoulders are back and there is a spring to his step. He looks as if he might be an athlete. You'd think twice before picking on him.

3

Even the most simple body gestures can mean a lot. In the first picture (4a) the girl is reacting to a threat by holding up her hands in a posture of helplessness. She looks terrified. Note (4b) the complete change that takes place when she does nothing more than turn her hands. She may know absolutely nothing about judo or karate, but her stance suggests that she is capable of defending herself. Chances are, her would be attacker will decide to back off.

In addition to the effective use of body language, there are basic common-sense precautions that will keep you out of trouble.

4a   4b

1. **Be Prepared.** Keep yourself in good physical condition. Take your gym classes seriously. Participate in competitive sports. Get into exercising, running, jogging, and the like.

2. **Stay Awake!** Keep yourself alert mentally. Walk with your eyes open and know what is going on around you. Develop a sense of smell

for danger. The football player who scores the most touchdowns is the one who runs fastest from his tacklers. A combination of physical and mental alertness are essential ingredients of self-confidence.

3. Maintain Your Space. The principle of territoriality applies to individual behavior. Did you ever notice that when you stand talking with someone, you instinctively maintain a comfortable distance? You can think of this distance as being your *space*.

When someone violates this space, as illustrated in photo (5), you immediately feel threatened. Conversely, you can get yourself into trouble by invading someone else's space.

5

Don't get too close to strangers. Girls in particular have to be careful. By thoughtlessly moving too close to someone, you may give the impression you're looking for attention.

By maintaining your space you also protect yourself from unexpected attack. This is particularly important in crowded public places such as subway platforms and on school buses. School buses, with crowds and noise, are good places for fights to break out. Anticipate trouble and be prepared to get away from it in one piece.

4. Be Cautious. Imagine you're a purse-snatcher and that you spot the girl pictured above. She's offering you a perfect target. One quick tug and her bag will be yours.

Six Simple Safety Precautions

* When shopping and paying for your purchase, don't flash your money. The person waiting in line behind you might be scouting for just such an opportunity.

* If you are carrying something particularly valuable, keep it secure in an inner pocket. If your wallet is lifted, you will then lose only items of secondary importance.

* In an elevator, stand near the button panel and know exactly where the alarm button is located.

* Before getting into your car, make sure that no one is hiding in the back seat.

* Drive with the door-lock buttons down, and don't pick up strangers.

* Get into the habit of traveling in pairs, whether it be on the sidewalk or in your school corridors. Never study alone in an empty classroom.

It's impossible, of course, to take every precaution. If you tried you'd become a complete paranoid, living under the constant delusion that everybody is out to get you. That's crazy. Instead, you must try to strike a happy balance through the use of normal good judgment.

In short, protect yourself with common sense.

·4·
FIVE WAYS TO STOP A FIGHT

You're at a school dance and all of a sudden there's a lot of noise. One of the kids is trying to start a fight, and if something isn't done quickly there could be a riot. Is there anything that you can do to calm the situation? Certainly you don't want to cripple someone with a karate chop. You only want to restrain him and, if necessary, remove him from the premises.

This is what is meant by an *arrest*. The purpose of an arrest is to control someone, hopefully without hurting him. Pain results only if he resists, and in this case he is actually hurting himself.

This chapter describes five strategies which are effective, yet easy to learn.

1. The Seat of the Pants Maneuver. This method of throwing out an unwanted guest is not very gracious, but it does the trick very nicely. It might not work if the subject is much stronger than you unless, of course, he's drunk.

The trick, as you can see from picture (6), is to grab the back of his collar with one hand, and the seat of his pants or his belt with the other. By pushing forward at the neck and pulling upward at his bottom, you can keep him pointed forward in an off-balance position. You will find it easy to walk him out, and you will hurt nothing but his dignity.

6

2. The Nightstick Walk-Away. Here you can use an umbrella, a cane, or anything else as a substitute for a nightstick. In the illustrations a meter stick is being used.

You approach the subject from the rear, the stick tucked beneath your armpit (7a-7b). As you come alongside, hook your arm under his and grasp the front of the stick (7c).

Now, quickly grab his wrist with your other hand and, using the stick as a lever, twist his arm outward against the normal bend of his elbow (7d). You can hurt him as much as you need to keep him quiet. Once he sees how helpless he is, you'll have no trouble leading him away.

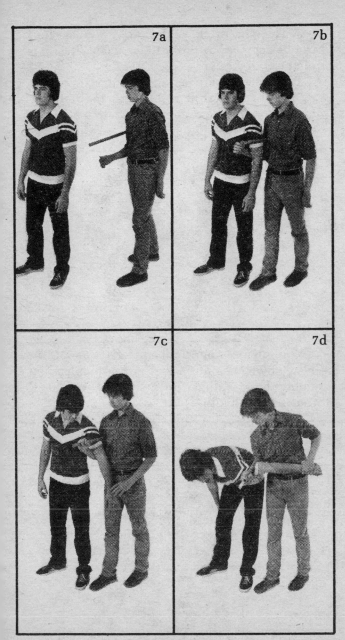

7a

7b

7c

7d

3. The Nightstick Variation. A similar effect can be achieved without the use of a stick. It is pictured in sequence (8).

This time you are facing the subject. Grab his right wrist with your right hand and pull him toward you, at the same time twisting his inner arm upward (8a).

8a

Now, pivot to your right and lace your left arm over, down, and under his arm. Complete the motion by grasping your own right wrist with your left hand (8b).

8b

As you can see in photo (8b), your left arm is now serving the role of the stick in sequence 7. Study this picture and you can see the advantage that you have. You can exert a much stronger downward pressure with your right arm than he can return upward with his trapped arm. Too much resistance could result in a painful dislocation of his elbow. He'll be happy to walk out with you.

4. The Break-a-Leg Maneuver. In show business the expression "break a leg" is a way of wishing someone good luck. As used here, the term is not quite so friendly.

This strategy works if you are able to bring the subject face downward on the floor. Rather than trying to hold him there with a cowboy saddle-hold, aim your attention at one of his legs. Set yourself so that one of your legs rests on the back of his knee joint. Then hook his foot in the crook of your arm, and force his lower leg back against your own leg.

As you can see by studying the picture (9), you can easily exert painful pressure against his knee joint. You can hold him in this position until someone comes along to give you a hand.

5. The Hammerlock. In a public place you prefer to remove a troublemaker without attracting too much attention. In order to do this, the hammerlock is an ideal hold. You can lead someone out of the place and make it look like you are the best of buddies.

The hold has to be applied quickly. You grab the subject's wrist and pull him toward you. Then circle around and behind him, pinning his arm behind his back. At the same time, hold his left arm to keep him from pulling away. In this position, any upward pressure on his arm will cause severe pain. You should have no trouble walking him away, arm in arm, in a very friendly way.

The five arrests described in this chapter are just a few of the many that you could learn. Try to master too many strategies, however, and you will remember none of them.

But master these five, and you'll feel a whole lot safer and more secure.

·5·
BLOCKING THE ATTACK

If you are set upon by an ordinary mugger, chances are the attack will follow one of a few basic patterns. Because these attacks usually come by surprise, you must learn to respond to them instinctively. This requires practice. The effort is worthwhile, however, because once the initial move is blocked, you will then be able to take command.

1. The Tackle Block. You are standing flat-footed and your attacker is rushing at you, arms spread ready to tackle. You know you have a second to absorb the force of his rush and keep from being thrown backward onto the ground. How do you do it?

It's not as difficult as it might seem. The trick is to meet his tackle with a mild one of your own. First, bend your shoulders, scooping your arms underneath his shoulders (10a). Then, at the instant that contact is made, throw your legs back as shown in (10b).

10 a

10 b

Note: The soles of your feet should be flat on the ground. You want to slide like one of the sleds that linemen push around in football practice. In this way you will absorb the force of the rush, and at the same time you will maintain an upright position. And once you have brought your foe to a halt, you are in a good position to apply a headlock or a number of other holds.

2. The Cover-Up. Muhammad Ali, the "greatest" of boxing champions, knows more than a little about blocking attacks. One of his

talents, most exciting to watch, has been his ability to lean back on the ropes, cover his face and body with his arms and gloves, and allow his opponent to flail away at him.

His strategy is simple. He allows his opponent to exhaust himself by delivering blows which don't hurt a bit.

You can employ the same strategy if you are set upon. Observe that the boy in the picture 11 is crouched in a purely defensive posture. Most of the punches thrown at him will be caught by his hands, arms, and shoulders.

11

If you can hold this position for a short time and dance away from your opponent's punches, he will soon grow tired. Only in the movies, brawlers never exhaust themselves.

When you take this crouching stance, however, be sure not to close your eyes, a natural instinct when someone is swinging at you. It's hard to do, but you have to train yourself to keep your eyes on your opponent, always searching for an opportunity. And when you see that his arms are getting heavy, you know it's time to make your move.

3. Block That Kick. If you get into a fight, it's a basic rule never to present a frontal target to your foe. Even in the boxing ring where kicking is not allowed, boxers tend to approach their opponents in a sideways manner before squaring off to deliver punches.

In karate, where kicking is allowed, the fighting stance is completely different, as you can see from picture (12). Notice the boy is ready to defend himself against either a punch or a kick. There is a springlike tension in his legs which will permit him to leap forward if he sees an opening, or backward if he wants to escape a blow.

12

It takes a lot of training to defend against karate kicks. Chances are, however, that a street brawler will use the "football punt" variety of kick. This is an easy kick to defend yourself against. If you are alert enough, all you have to do is back away from it.

Once you have dodged the kick, you are in command. Study the first picture (12a) in the sequence and note that the aggressor is completely off balance. You could hurt him badly if you threw a quick tackle at his only supporting leg. This is why football rules prohibit the charging of the kicker. No such rules apply, however, in self-defense. Feel completely free to give your attacker a lesson in the benefits of maintaining proper balance.

The sequence of pictures shows an alternative defense, one in which you don't have to hit the ground yourself.

Catch his foot at the height of its swing, (12b), then step up and hook your heel behind his grounded foot. A slight push will now topple him onto his back, (12c).

12 a

12b

4. The Club Attack. If someone comes at you swinging a club, you are in serious trouble, and your best defense is a hasty exit. A hard blow almost anywhere on your head or neck could kill you.

But what if you don't get the chance to run? What are your chances for survival? Not as bad as you might think.

The first thing to do is stop the swing before it builds up enough strength to break through your block. If possible, grab the club with both hands, as shown in the first picture (13a). Study this picture carefully and note the position of the attacker's thumb. The thumb has practically no strength, and by using the force of both your arms, you can twist against the thumb and break the club free (13b).

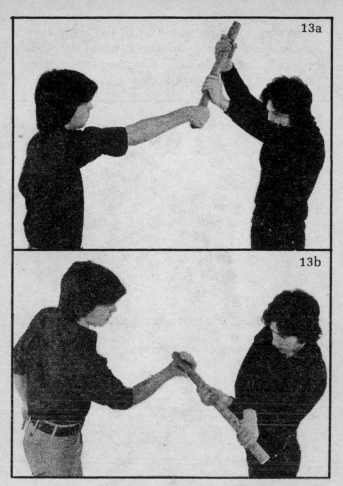

13a

13b

It's a lot more difficult to defend yourself if your foe plunges the club at you. Here you must pull back to escape the blow, and at the same time grab the club with both your hands.

Once you have done this, *do not engage in a tug-of-war*. Instead, employ the judo principle of using your enemy's own strength to floor him. Pull the club in the direction it is already moving, toward you. This will increase your opponent's momentum, and he will fly neatly over the leg block which you have conveniently provided. Not only will he find himself sprawled on the ground, but you will own a new club.

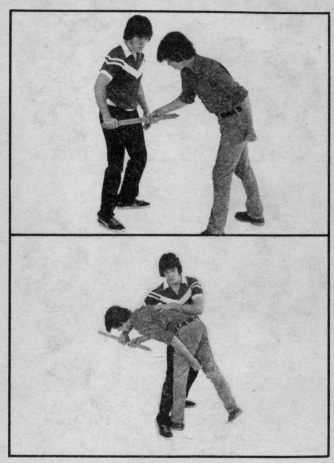

5. The Wrist Pull. A typical move by a bully is to grab the wrists of a person weaker than himself. If this has ever happened to you, you know how humiliating it can be.

Your immediate reaction is to resist by pulling in the opposite direction. This only makes things worse unless you yourself are just as strong. Instead, use the same judo principle mentioned before.

For a brief moment, try to pull away. This will cause your foe to double his own effort. The moment he does, throw yourself at him. Now his own strength is being used to throw himself backward to the ground, and you will land on top of him. If, as you fall, your knee should happen to dig into the pit of his stomach, don't apologize. He'll feel better in a week or two.

6. How to Survive a Brawl. You are at a dance and all of a sudden a free-for-all breaks out. What do you do? Riot scenes are perhaps the most dangerous of all because there is no logic to people's behavior. Carried away by frenzy, they swing away at anyone and everyone. Your first instinct should be to look for the nearest exit.

However, if you are trapped in the middle of a melee, you should try to find yourself a corner and square yourself off so that attack can come from only one direction. Grab a chair if you can, and use it like a lion tamer, to ward off lunges and as a weapon as well. If you are dating, the girl should be cornered behind the guy so that no direct assault can be made against her.

If things get real bad and you are hurt or unable to fight, your best defense is that of the turtle. Outwardly it might look like you're being a coward, but if it saves your life you can worry about that the following day.

Fall to the floor on your side, then tuck your knees up under your chin. This will protect your stomach and chest. Clasp your hands behind your neck, and bring your elbows around to cover your face. This will cover the vital areas of your head and neck. In the fracas you might suffer a few kicks, but it is unlikely that someone will take the trouble to unwind you in order to deliver a blow.

You might even save yourself by feigning unconsciousness. Unless a person is insane, he will not try to hurt someone who is already subdued.

Needless to say, your best free-for-all defense is to stay away from places where such a scene might occur.

• 6 •
GREAT ESCAPES

You are walking home from school. Suddenly, someone grabs you from behind. Maybe it's just one of your friends playing a joke. On the other hand, it might be someone who is really trying to hurt you. In either case, one thing is sure. You want to get free. That's what this chapter is about—how to escape.

There are many ways in which someone might grab you, and once again, you can't memorize every possible means of escape. As we have done before, we'll concentrate on the few holds that are the most common.

The escapes described in this chapter are weaponless. Let's face it, you don't want to kill or cripple a classmate just because he loses his temper and grabs you. At such times you want to show him who's boss without resorting to violence. At the same time, you want to pack a wallop if the threat should be serious.

The basic rule is to stay calm. The wilder the attack, the easier it is to deflect it, if you are in control of yourself. Instead of yielding to panic, take a deep breath, brace yourself, and try to figure out the best way of getting out of this mess.

In any escape you want to muster as much strength as you can. Just before making your move, take a deep breath. Then, exhale quickly and hard as you make your move.

This is a well-known trick, and it explains all the grunts and shouts that you hear in wrestling and karate matches. It is even good to scream like a banshee while fighting off an attack. In addition to gaining more strength, you might also frighten and confuse your foe.

1. Wrist Holds. In the last chapter we talked a bit about wrist holds. It is humiliating to be powerless in someone else's grip. Your inability to escape is a sign of weakness, and makes your tormentor feel even more tough.

The plain truth is, wrist holds are easy to break. You simply have to remember one simple principle: *work against the thumbs.* The strength of a handgrip, you see, lies in the fingers, and the thumb makes a very small contribution. For this reason you can use the thumb as your escape hatch.

There are so many ways someone can grab your wrists that total confusion would result if you tried to memorize an escape for each. For this reason we will consider only two possible situations. Both illustrate the principle of breaking through the thumbs.

Look at photos (15a-15b). The boy has grabbed the girl's left wrist with his right hand. Notice his thumb is pointed downward. In order to set herself free, the girl simply has to swing her arm in an outward and downward arc with sufficient strength to force open his thumb. If his thumb had been pointed upward, she would have swung her arm in an inward and downward arc.

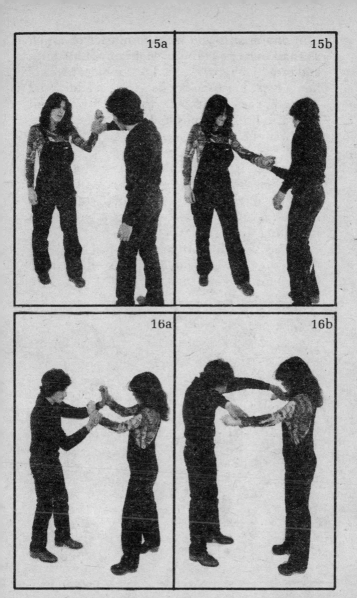

15a 15b

16a 16b

The second pair of photos (16a-16b) shows
the girl being held by both wrists. She could
never escape by pulling away. Her first move is

41

to kick at his shins, forcing him to back away. This takes some of the strength out of his grip, and provides her with the right moment to make her move. Clenching her fists to gain additional strength, she swings both arms downward and outward. If his thumbs had been in a different position she would adjust her swing accordingly.

The description sounds much more complicated than the escapes themselves. With a little practice you will find that the moves come quite naturally, and you will develop a rhythm in executing them.

2. The Bear Hug. Anyone who has ever been the victim of an unwanted embrace will want to know how to break this hold.

The first pair of pictures (17a-17b) show you what to do if you are being held from the front. Instead of pulling back, which is the normal reaction, step up to your foe and hook your foot behind his heels. Now cup the heel of your right hand beneath his nose and push upward and back until he either lets go or topples backward. You can hasten his fall by pulling on his shirt sleeve. If he is foolish enough to hold on to you as he falls, be sure to land on him knees first.

It is harder to break a bear hug from the rear. You might do it by stomping as hard as you can on one of his feet. If your lower arms are free you could also use the points of your hands to hit at his kidneys.

The best surprise move, however, is shown in the two pictures (18a-18b). Bend your body forward as if you were trying to touch your toes. Then reach back through your legs and grab the cuffs of his pants. Hold on tight, straighten yourself upward, and listen for the thud behind you!

18a   18b

3. The Strangle. As a form of attack, the strangle would most likely come from someone who is a maniac. Hopefully there aren't too many of these in your circle of friends. You can imagine, however, the horror of such a threat. In a matter of seconds you could be unconscious. Nonetheless, the situation is not as bad as it may seem.

FRONT: If the hold is from the front, lean to the right and clasp your hands. Then, as if you were swinging a sledgehammer, swing your stiffened arms over and through his arms in a wide arc, as the girl is demonstrating in the photo series (19a-19d). If her attacker doesn't let go, his left arm will be broken at the elbow.

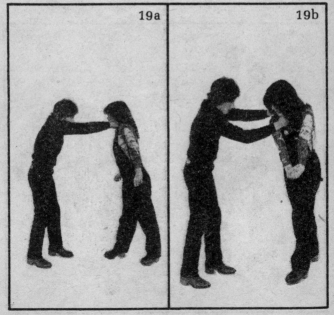

19a   19b

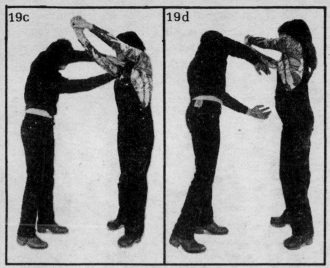

Another way to escape is shown in the pair of photos (20a-20b). Clench your hands in front of you so they form a single fist, (20a). Then swing both arms in an upward and outward thrust, (20b). This will spread his arms outward and break his grip on you.

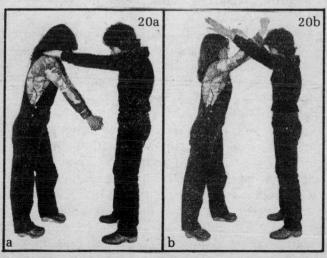

REAR: If anyone ever tries to strangle you from the rear, you might break his grip by grabbing a little finger in each of your fists and twisting them outward. If your attacker is very strong, however, this might not work.

A better choice, shown in photos (21a-21b), is to throw up your right arm and spin to the right at the same time. The strength of your arm and shoulder should be enough to break the hold, as you can see in the second picture above. If you take a second look at this picture, you will note also that your left hand will be in a good position to deliver a blow to his neck with your pointed left hand.

What if you're walking home from a late movie and someone comes up behind you and hooks his arm around your neck? Photo (22a) shows what we mean. How do you handle that situation? You'll have no trouble if you learn a maneuver that they teach in judo classes.

First, as in (22b), jab your right elbow back into the pit of his stomach. This will cause him to double back, and he will be off balance. Now grab his elbow and his upper arm as shown in the third photo (22c). Note that your knees should be bent slightly. From this position you make one sharp motion, straightening your legs and bending forward, at the same time pulling hard on his upper arm. If this is done correctly, your opponent will fly over your shoulder and land on his back at your feet (22d).

Don't practice this kind of a throw, however, unless you and your partner have had some instruction in the art of falling correctly. This takes considerable practice. In essence, the trick is to slap one or both of your arms hard against the mat at the moment that you hit. This has the effect of absorbing the force of the fall. However, do not attempt this or any other throw without further instruction. This book teaches self-defense, not self destruction!

4. The Headlock. You're in the locker room and a bunch of guys are horsing around. The next thing you know some character has you in a headlock. It's all in fun, but at the same time you're being put down, and you don't like it. You'd like to have the reputation of being someone to respect. Can you handle it?

In a situation like this, the best defense is often the simplest. A sharp elbow dig to the stomach will convince your "friend" you don't like his brand of humor.

If the attack is a genuine act of violence you can take firmer measures. Notice in the first photo in sequence (23) how close the attacker's hand is to his victim's mouth. You have sharp teeth and strong jaws. Don't be ashamed to use them. If the king of the jungle can bite, why shouldn't you?

In an ordinary schoolyard scuffle, of course, biting is definitely out. But there is no such thing as dirty fighting if you are fighting for your life.

The second photo (23b), shows a less drastic way of breaking a headlock. You grab the attacker's wrist with your left hand and circle his waist with your right arm. Then bring your right knee into the joint of his left knee. In this position you can cause severe pain by bending your knee into the joint. If he doesn't let go of you, he'll have a broken leg.

23

23b

5. The Rear Arm-Lock. If you aren't too strong, this is a difficult hold to break free from. The most obvious defense is to use your feet. You can stomp on one of his feet, kick back at his shin, or scrape his shin with the heel of your shoe. If this doesn't get you free, your foe will at least be forced to pull back a bit, as shown in the second photo below. This provides your opportunity. Look closely at sequence (24). Twist slightly to the left, clasp your hands, and stiffen your arms. Then spin your body and swing your arms in a right circular motion to face him. Your arms will break his hold and you will be free.

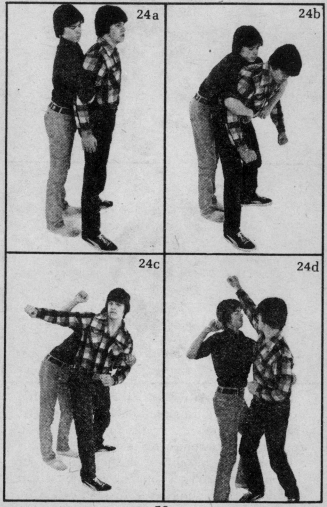

Using Pressure Points

Imagine this: You are pinned to the ground by a guy who is twice your size. In the background you can hear a few people laughing at your helplessness. A few seconds later their amusement turns into amazement because you are now standing free.

Sound impossible? Far from it! You can do amazing things if you know about the pressure points of the human body.

As an example, you can find two such points by placing your thumbs below your jaw and moving them back toward your neck. Just before you come to the neck, you will find two hollows. Press gently into these hollows, and you will get an idea of how sensitive they are.

A very sensitive point is the under part of the nose. There isn't a man alive whom you can't force backward merely by pushing beneath the nose with your index finger. In a fight it is often possible to cup your opponent's nose in your hand and push upward with the heel of your palm. He'll be off you pronto!

The back of the hand is also sensitive. If someone is holding you, you can get away by digging the knuckle of your middle finger into the back of his hand. You'll also find out how loud he can shout.

It is said that Oriental combat experts know more about the human body than most doctors. This may be true, but certainly your needs are not that demanding. It will be enough if you know just a few points. First locate them on your own body, and then with your partner practice finding them quickly in simulated combat.

Front Body Pressure Points:

- The depressions under the cheekbones
- Below the armpits, just under the biceps
- The neck hollow just above the collarbone
- The Adam's apple

Rear Body Pressure Points:

- The hollows behind the knees
- A couple inches right and left of the back of the neck, halfway down
- The hollows between the inside ankles and Achilles' tendons

In a struggle the worst thing that you can do is to waste your strength punching at fatty or muscular areas of your opponent's body. He might be black-and-blue a couple days later, but then it will be too late to do you any good. Instead, you must direct your blows at sensitive areas where the pain will be immediate.

· 7 ·
THE KNIFE ATTACK

You are walking home from your date's house on a dark street and you see an unpleasant looking stranger walking in your direction. Something about his manner makes you uncomfortable. Before you know it he is close and you hear the click of a switchblade and see the glint of steel. What experience could be more frightening? The thought of being stabbed is enough to send shivers down anyone's spine.

Hopefully you will never have such an encounter. The seriousness of a knife attack, however, is sufficient to command your careful study of this chapter.

The first rule is to get away if you can, as fast as you can. When you are face-to-face with a dangerous animal, there is no disgrace in running like mad. A girl wearing awkward shoes should kick them off in order to get maximum speed. Shoes can be replaced, a life can't.

If you can't escape by running away, your next option is to use your head. Unless your attacker is a maniac, his primary purpose is to scare, not cut you. He has some other purpose. Does he want your money? Give it to him! Don't risk your life for a few dollars.

Should you scream for help? There is no sure answer to this question, because no two situations are the same. One mugger might be frightened off by a scream, whereas another might panic and lunge at you. What's more, screams don't always bring help. Not too long ago a woman died screaming on a street in New York City while her neighbors, paralyzed with fear, watched from nearby windows.

If you do scream, you might shout "Fire!" rather than "Help!" People love to watch fires, and you might draw a crowd very quickly.

Remember too that your attacker is quite possibly off his rocker. If it seems at all possible, try to soothe him with warm words, much as you would try to calm a snarling dog. Even if you feel that you can handle the situation, make your attacker think you are afraid. This may cause him to relax, giving you an opportunity to strike.

Stall for time and try to maneuver yourself into a position of advantage. A rule of battle is to try to occupy the high ground. Don't allow yourself to be backed into a corner. If any kind of makeshift weapon is within reach, grab it. The lid of a garbage can could become a life-saving shield. Indoors, pick up a chair and use it in the fashion of a lion tamer. In a later chapter, on the use of weapons, you will find more good suggestions for just such a situation.

Remember: When being threatened with a dangerous weapon, your life is on the line. You can forget all the rules of fair play. Use any weapon, clean or dirty. Deliver any blow, high or low. Your foe deserves no consideration.

If you can't get away, you have to meet the attack with maximum efficiency. Your first job is to arrest the swing. Always try to block the wrist, not the weapon. Don't try, however, to catch his wrist with your hand. It's too easy to miss. Instead, cross your wrists, fingers tightly outstretched, as shown in photo (25). Catch the attacker's wrist in the V formed by your own wrists. Try to make the catch early in the swing before too much momentum builds up. This block will work with any kind of swing except the straight lunge which, as you will see later, requires a special strategy.

25

How To Practice
This Chapter

Here's how you and your partner should practice. Roll a single sheet of composition paper, and let that be the knife. Do not use a fake knife or a stick. These are capable of doing plenty of damage.

Take turns at being the aggressor and the victim. Practice the block over and over, varying the direction of the swing, until you both have it down cold. Remember, enough practice could save your life.

Once you have blocked the swing, you are far from being out of the woods. You still have a knife to deal with, and taking a knife away from someone is anything but easy. If you have any other alternative, take it. A strong kick, for example, might disable your foe for a minute and give you the chance to run.

You'll have to practice long hours before you are good enough to disarm a person with a blade. The following instructions are fairly standard with most experts in self-defense. They vary depending on the direction of the thrust.

1. The Overhand Swing. This attack would most likely come from someone who has had no training in knife fighting. It is the easiest to defend against. As soon as you have caught the attacker's wrist in the V of your own wrists (26a), grab his wrist with your right hand, thumb pointed downward, and twist so that the under part of his arm is up (26b). Now, step up, hook your left arm over and around his arm (26c), and grab your right wrist with your left hand (26d).

26a

26b

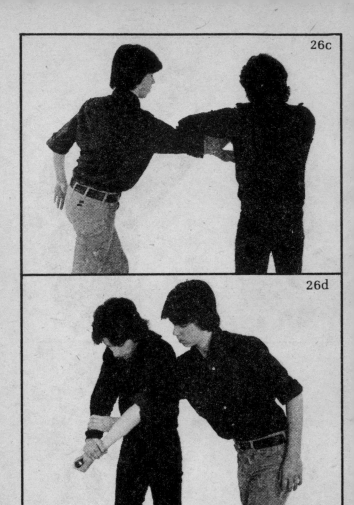

26c

26d

Carefully study your position in the photo
sequence above. In this position (26d), you have
a tremendous physical advantage. Your left arm
is a crowbar pressing against your opponent's
elbow joint.

CAUTION: Only a small amount of pressure
from your right hand can cause much pain, too
much pressure could break an arm. Be very care-

ful when practicing this with your partner, especially when you're getting good and fast. Don't forget, this is practice.

2. The Cross-Body Slash. From the first picture in sequence (27), you can see the path that the swing will follow. Again, you must first block the swing in the V of your wrists. As with the overhand swing, grab his wrist with your right hand and follow the same procedure. Once he has dropped the knife you can maintain the hold until help arrives.

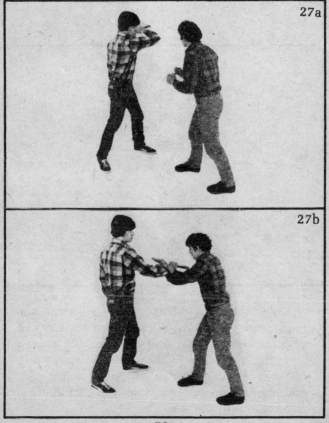

27a

27b

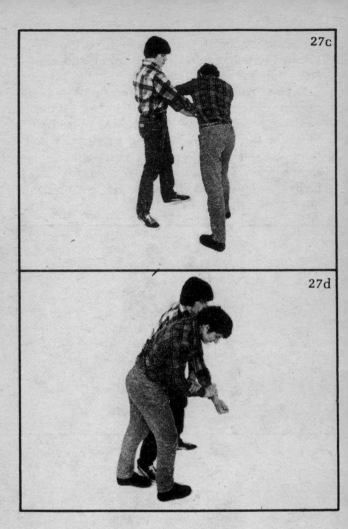

27c

27d

3. The Underhand Swing. This is a tough one to get away from. You catch his wrist in the V of your own wrists (28a), and you grasp his wrist in your right hand. Now, however, there is a big difference. As you can see from the photo, you're not in a good position to safely circle his arm with your left arm.

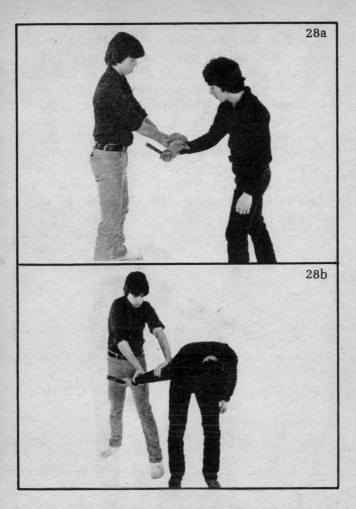

28a

28b

Instead you must jerk his arm toward you and downward. This will put him off balance. At the same time that you pull, twist his wrist to the right and clamp your left hand on his elbow, as in photo (28b). You now have all the strength of your left arm to work against his elbow joint. Using pressure, you can force him to the ground and hold him there until help comes.

4. The Straight Thrust. Take a long look at photo (29), below. It illustrates the stance of a trained knife-fighter. The point of the knife is directed straight at the foe, blade up. The wrist is locked so that the knife has become an extension of the arm. When a thrust is made, the knifer has the advantage of the full length of his arm and the knife combined. His left hand is in position to parry any counterattack. If he were fighting another knifer, his left hand would be wrapped in a jacket or some other item to protect it from being cut.

29

Never attempt a weaponless defense against such a threat. Your chance for survival would be almost nil. Give him anything reasonable that he asks for. Only if it becomes clear that his prime intent is to hurt you should you attempt to block his blows or disable him.

Grab any object that will serve as a shield or as a weapon. If you can deflect the thrust, perhaps you'll be close enough to deliver a strong kick. If his face looms close, thrust something at his eyes. If you can hurt him even for a moment, you might be able to get away.

You and your partner will have to spend a lot of time working together before you become even remotely good at knife defense. Your goal is to reach the point where every reaction is instinctive. Under attack you don't have time to think.

A final point is unpleasant to consider but necessary. When defending yourself against a knifer, your primary goal is to stay in one piece. (No pun intended.) You must prevent an attacker from getting too close. In the process, you might get a cut on your hand or your arm. You must not panic at the sight of your own blood. If you lose the clarity of your mind, you stand no chance.

How can you achieve such mental control? Oriental philosophy teaches it through concentration and meditation. You might do it through ordinary willpower and the instinct for survival.

Hopefully, however, you will never have to use any of the skills that you have learned from this chapter.

· 8 ·
YOUR BODY WEAPONS

You and your friends are leaving the football stadium. Your school team has just won the game, and everyone is feeling good and horsing around. Then, before you know what is happening, you're surrounded by a gang of kids from the other school. They couldn't win the game on the field, so they're going to try to do it on the sidewalk.

In such a set-up you have no choice but to stand your ground and fight back. And you have many weapons that you can use, weapons that you carry with you all the time. They belong to your body.

When most people are attacked they usually react with defenses that are inadequate, or with blows that are ineffective. Sometimes it works, sometimes it doesn't. If you want to escape this mistake, study this chapter well.

But first, a word of caution. You and your partner should never strike an actual blow at each other. Instead use an old mattress, discarded cushions, or the like. If you do practice with each other, learn to pull your punches. Even in a karate match, actual blows never land.

Try this for some practice look at photos below. Practice your punches on a basketball. The distance the ball travels will tell you how effective your blows are. Make a contest out of it. See who can make the basketball travel the farthest.

Finally, as you go through this chapter remember one important thing. Effective self-defense never looks anything like the wild, arm-flailing, chair-throwing, rail-leaping brawls in the movies. *The most effective blows are the ones that can't be seen.*

1.The Clenched Fist. This is the fighting fist that is standard in Western culture. As shown in photo (31), the grip must be tight. The fingers must be tucked in so no bone will snap on contact. The thumb should never be tucked inside the fingers.

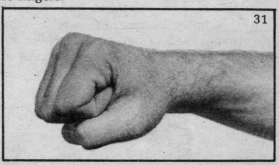

31

Check your wrist. Is it straight and solid? Unless the wrist is locked perfectly straight into the fist, there will be nothing behind your punch. Worse still, your wrist could break.

If your wrists are weak, strengthen them by pumping an ordinary rubber ball in each hand, as explained in the chapter, "Keeping Fit."

The clenched fist is most effective against the soft stomach or the vulnerable face. More often than not, a bloody nose is usually the end of a fight. A good punch to the jaw can knock someone out, usually without any permanent damage. However, the clenched fist does not offer the best use of the hand in self-defense situations.

2. The Pointed Fist. As you can see from photo (32), this is the clenched fist with one important difference. The knuckle of your middle finger is pointed out, clamped into position by the thumb. Again, be careful all your fingers are tucked in securely, and that your wrist is locked tightly to the fist.

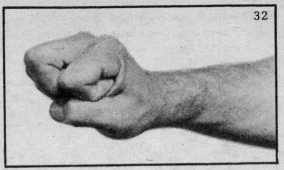

32

The pointed fist is very effective when used against your opponent's body. This is because the entire force of your blow is concentrated in a single point.

Aimed at the throat, the blow from the pointed fist can be lethal. Be careful about how serious a threat is; there is no reason to hurt anyone more than necessary to protect yourself.

3. **The Pointed Hand.** As you can see from the photo, the pointed hand offers much the same advantage as the pointed fist. You can use it effectively against the throat and the soft stomach and kidney regions. However, don't use it against the head or the muscular regions of your foe, because one of your own fingers can break. (Photo 33a)

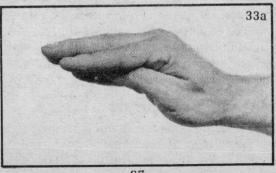

33a

4. The Blade of the Hand. This is the hand position used in karate chop. Note from the picture that the hand should be slightly cupped, not straight (33b).

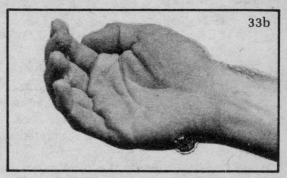

33b

Breaking Bricks
With Your Hand: DON'T

Everyone has seen karate demonstrations in which experts use the blade of the hand to break wooden planks and bricks. Don't try this yourself, however, unless you want to get to know the emergency ward of your nearest hospital. It takes years to toughen the hand and to discipline the mind to the degree that makes such feats possible.

The blade of the hand can be extremely effective, however, even with a minimal amount of practice. A blow to the side of the neck will knock someone out. If the blow is hard enough it could rupture an artery, and death would result. Again, learn to separate a schoolyard fight from a life and death threat.

5. The Heel of the Hand. As illustrated in photo (34), the heel of the hand is most effective when used in an uppercut swing to the point of the chin or the tip of the nose. **CAUTION: A shot**

against the nose can kill. It should be used only in a life and death situation. Practice on a basketball, not on a friend.

34

A good punch is a lot more than just throwing your fist at someone. To get the most out of a punch, you must make it *short*, *fast*, and *forceful*. Let's take a look at each of these factors.

If you wind up to deliver a long punch, as in photo (35), your foe will have no trouble ducking it. A good punch should travel just a short distance. Your opponent has no chance of escaping it.

35

An untrained fighter usually can't punch fast *and* hard. You can increase your power by tensing your muscles, but this will make you lose your speed. On the other hand, if you loosen up your muscles to get speed, your punch will pack no wallop.

How do you throw a fast, hard punch? Try this. Throw the punch with your muscles completely loosened, giving you speed, and then tense your muscles at the exact moment of contact. This way you get both speed and power. Home-run hitters know this trick well. Learning it requires a lot of practice, but the results will make it worthwhile. You'll be astounded at how far that basketball can fly.

6. The Foot. No one has to tell you you can hurt someone pretty badly with a well-aimed kick. In karate demonstrations, experts use their feet as much as their hands. You are no expert, however, and you have to learn one important *don't* about kicking.

36a

Don't make the mistake in photo (36a). If his kick had landed the fight would be over. But he missed. You don't even need a second picture to know what is going to happen next. The other guy simply has to grab his foot and flip him to the ground.

If you do kick, make it short and sweet. And try to divert his attention so that he doesn't see it coming. In photo (36b)the girl has thrown her sweater into her attacker's face, and is about to kick at his sensitive shin.

Kicking, of course, is justified only in genuine cases of self-defense. In a routine schoolyard fight, kicking is definitely "dirty" fighting.

Stay-away kicks are a good defense for a girl who is being annoyed. Shin scraping is a good way to say "no" to unwanted embrace, as shown in photo (37). Notice how when someone's been kicked, the tendency is to bend forward, making the face a target for a second blow. This is called the high-low strike system, or "the old one-two."

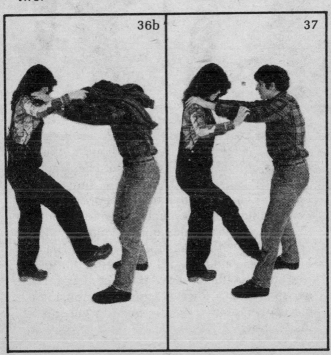

36b

37

You should also learn to use your foot as a hook. If you watch a judo demonstration you'll see what this means. The key strategy of judo is to break your opponent's balance. The photo sequence (38a-38b) gives a good illustration of this.

Notice how the boy sneaks his right foot behind the heel of his opponent. From this position he merely has to twist his body to the left and his opponent will pitch over backward.

Finally, something called "the dancer's defense." Ever had your toes stepped on accidently? Imagine how much more harm you can cause with a deliberate stomp! In photo (39), the boy being held looks helpless. Not so. His feet are free, and a downward blow will get himself free and provide the entertainment of an Indian dance as well. However, this isn't considered too cool unless you really need to get free no matter how.

7. The Knee. The use of the knee is usually associated with dirty fighting. In real-life self-defense, however, anything goes.

In addition to the obvious frontal attack, the knee can be used in other ways. In photo (40a) the boy is using his knees to collapse the legs of his opponent, making it easy to bring him to the ground. In the second picture (40b), the knee is being used as a restraining weapon to keep an aggressor pinned to the ground.

40a

If you yourself are on the ground, on your back, and someone is about to jump on you, a raised knee will make his landing somewhat uncomfortable.

8. The Elbow. Ask any football lineman, particularly a center, how much an elbow punch can hurt. The elbow packs a lot of power.

If someone is holding you from behind, a sharp backward dig can set you free. The effect is even better if you are shorter than your foe.

If you are being held from the front, an across-the-body roundhouse with your elbow could easily rearrange your captor's dental structure. A swing with the elbow is backed by the strong muscles of your shoulder and upper arm. And once your swing is completed, your elbow is in position for a return trip, as you can see in the pictures in sequence (41).

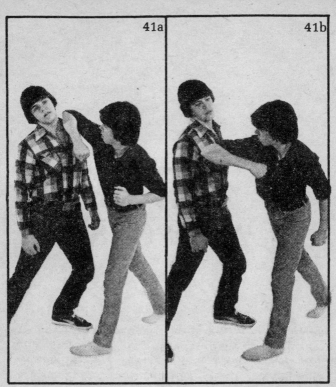

41a

41b

9. Using Your Head. Your head is hard and heavy. If you are being held from the rear and you are the same height as your foe, a quick backward swing of your head could land on his nose and give him enough pain to make him let go. In a tackle, your head makes a good battering ram.

Your head is best employed, however, when you use the brain that is contained inside it. Studying this book is a step in the right direction. You will survive attack only if you are prepared to meet it. We often think of super-athletes as being all muscle, but any manager or coach will tell you that all the brawn in the world is worthless without a brain to direct it.

·9·
WEAPONS

Do you carry a knife? Have you ever seen a blackjack or a pair of brass knuckles? If you live or go to school in a tough neighborhood, it might seem the smart thing to protect yourself by carrying a weapon. Don't. You're making the biggest mistake of your life.

In the first place, it's against the law to carry an unlicensed concealed weapon. You could get picked up and get your name on police files. Even more serious, you might wound or kill someone. You might have been acting in defense, but you yourself could end up in jail. You might even be sued by your attacker or his family, strange as it may seem.

This doesn't mean that you don't have the right to defend your life. You do. But the law is very sensitive about the use of weapons. A jury might say that the very fact that you were armed was in itself a sign of aggressive intent.

When you defend yourself, the law does not allow you to use violence if there is any other way in which you could have escaped the danger. And if it is necessary to answer force with force, you are not allowed to use more force than that which threatens you. As an extreme example, you can't use a hammer to ward off an attack with a flyswatter. This restriction, coupled with the danger that you might over-react to a simple annoyance, could get you into a lot of trouble.

A further danger in arming yourself is the possibility that you yourself might get to be nasty. There is a feeling of power that comes from holding a weapon, and the urge to use it can become very strong. Every year youngsters who got air-guns for Christmas and couldn't resist the urge to try them out are arrested. From time to time even police officers have to be dismissed from the force because they can't handle the sense of power that comes from carrying a gun.

Your own peace of mind is at stake too. If you ever should seriously hurt someone in defending yourself and later find out the threat was not serious after all, you would live the rest of your life with feelings of regret and guilt.

Finally, like it or not, the fact that you are a teenager would work against you if you were ever caught carrying a weapon. The law takes a dim view of adolescents carrying weapons; at the very least, you'd probably get bounced from school.

Despite all the above, there are ways that you can arm yourself if an emergency calls for it. There are plenty of makeshift weapons which are effective. There's nothing wrong, for example, with carrying a ring of keys. Yet they can be turned into an efficient weapon.

In the remainder of the chapter you will learn how to turn some ordinary things into weapons, and how to use them effectively.

1. The Mighty Club. You are walking home from a late movie and the streets are deserted. Suddenly you hear someone coming up behind you. Perhaps there is no danger, but you can't afford to take a chance. You have to be prepared. Fortunately, you are carrying the magazine section from last Sunday's newspaper!

Does that sound crazy? Actually it isn't. It takes only a few moments to roll the paper into a tight cylinder, and presto! you have a formidable club! It won't do any damage in a downward swing, of course, but jam it into a predator's stomach and he'll get the clear message you don't want to be messed with.

Naturally you don't want to spend your entire life walking around with a club in your hand. Think of all the specific times, however, when the danger of attack is greater than usual. You might, for example, be involved in a school play, and one or two nights a week you might have a lonely walk home. At times such as these you should be prepared. Women, particularly, can defend themselves relatively easily if they are carrying an umbrella.

Experts in the use of the club, such as policemen with their nightsticks, rarely use them in hammer-like swings. An alert foe can too easily catch the club and take it away. Underhand thrusts and cross-body slashes are much more effective. And in delivering blows such as these, your rolled magazine is every bit as good as a piece of hickory.

In the photos in sequence (42), note that after the club is swung in one direction, it is in position for a return blow in the opposite direction. Again, the old "one-two." Note also that the club is held at the middle rather than at the end.

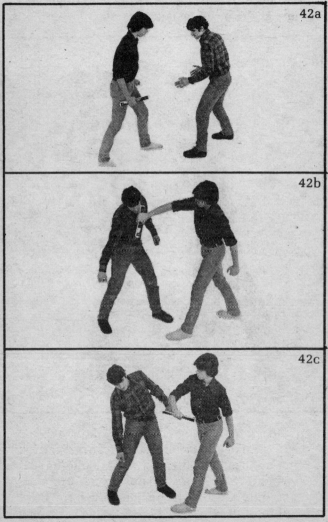

42a

42b

42c

Needless to say, don't practice these blows on your partner. Once again you can get the idea of the power of your makeshift club by using it on a basketball. Use the same delivery technique recommended for the fist punch. Keep your muscles loose during the swing, and then tense them at the exact instant of contact.

43a

Many people carry umbrellas, and they too make an excellent club which can be carried without attracting attention. In the photo (43a) above, however, the girl is using her umbrella incorrectly. Even if she hits her target, the blow wouldn't hurt anything bigger than a fly. Much better if she holds her umbrella as shown in (43b). The moment an aggresser gets close, she is ready to thrust the weapon into the pit of his stomach.

43b

2. Fist Helpers. Before every prizefight the officials carefully inspect the taped hands of the fighters. The officials know that even a small weight added to the fist will multiply the force of each punch.

If you are face to face with a mugger, there are no officials and no rules. A roll of pennies clenched in your fist could give you the extra power needed to deliver a knockout punch. Even a handful of loose change will do the trick. If trouble comes in a restaurant, an average sized salt shaker will serve the same purpose.

Do you carry a ring of keys? If you do you, can change your fist into a punishing medieval mace. As shown in photo (44), the keys are arranged so that they stick out between the fingers close to the knuckles. When the time comes that you have a car, this is a good practice to remember when you are walking through a lonely parking lot.

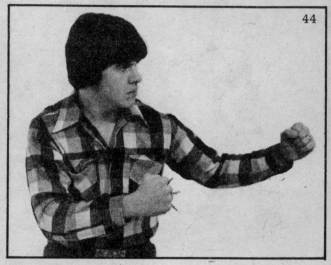

44

The next time you see a U.S. Marine in dress uniform, notice the large, handsome buckle he wears. If you have a relative or friend who served in the Marines, he will tell you that this buckle can be a powerful weapon. Chances are that you too have a belt with a large buckle, the kind that you wear with jeans.

The moment you sense trouble, remove your belt and wrap it around your hand until the buckle hangs loose by about six inches. As you can see from photo (45), the sight of such a weapon might make someone think twice before starting trouble.

45

3. Moment of Blindness. Talking about Marines, many of them learned a clever trick while fighting on the beaches during World War II. A handful of sand thrown into the eyes of an onemy con provide the few moments necessary to take him out.

You go to the beach just to enjoy the sun. If someone starts trouble, however, remember that you have a weapon right at your feet. If someone goes after you in a restaurant, a pepper shaker contains an eye irritant even better than sand.

For people who go out alone at night regularly, it's not a bad idea to carry a shaker of pepper, sealed of course, in your pocket or purse. When walking a lonely street, remove the cap and carry the shaker in your fist, sealing the top with your thumb. You will be ready to act at a moment's notice. And, you'll get away without a punch being thrown.

A ballpoint pen can be as lethal as a dagger. As shown in photo (46), it should be gripped between the index and middle fingers and braced in the thumb joint of your palm. *However, the use of such a weapon is extremely dangerous, and should be reserved only for times of extreme danger.* Again, learn to separate a shoving match from a real threat.

46

The use of weapons is not a pleasant topic, but being attacked isn't exactly fun either. There are times when you must stand your ground. Remember, all these weapons can really cause damage. They are not toys. A weapon can invite trouble as well as repel it. That's why most are illegal.

·10·
THE MARTIAL ARTS

You are surrounded by a dozen enemies. A few are armed with knives, and some are wielding chains. All of them are bigger than you, and they have only one thought—to kill.

You tense your body and wait for the right moment. Then, in movements too swift to be detected, you unleash your power. One by one your enemies fall as your body is transformed into a devastating machine of destruction. In a matter of minutes your foes are crumpled masses of flesh and broken bones.

Did you ever wake up from a dream like that? If you have, perhaps you have thought of joining a school of martial arts.

This book has made no attempt to teach any of the martial disciplines. Nonetheless, it's not a bad idea to take a few pages to explain what they're all about.

The martial arts go back in history as far as 5000 B.C. They originated in China and India, developed by travelers who needed to defend themselves against ambush on lonely roads and in treacherous mountain passes.

Moving up to the 1600's, it was against the law in Japan to carry weapons, and this created the need to take care of oneself without them. It wasn't until very recently that the Oriental systems became known in the United States.

The martial arts are divided into two categories, the hard arts and the soft arts. The former, including karate and kung fu, emphasize combat. The soft arts, on the other hand, put stress on body and mind coordination. These include t'ai chi ch'uan, aikido, and judo. When soft school disciples are attacked, they use the strength of the attacker against himself instead of returning blow for blow.

The most violent of the martial arts is kung fu, probably familiar to you because of movies and television. The softest of the martial arts is t'ai chi ch'uan, which puts mind and body in harmony through dancelike routines, practiced most often in privacy.

In most urban and suburban areas, there are a number of schools that you can choose from. The most common are ju-jitsu and karate, so we'll limit ourselves here to a brief look at these two.

All of the martial arts reject the use of weapons. The student depends entirely on the effective use of his or her body. The historical reason for this is more than aesthetic. Oriental peasants couldn't afford fancy swords, so they taught themselves to use their own bodies as weapons.

In fact, similar forms of fighting evolved in regions of the world far removed from Oriental influence. Loggers on the West Coast of the United States and trappers in remote regions of Canada developed systems of combat remarkably similar to judo and karate.

Ju-jitsu received attention in the United States during the early days of World War II. Japanese soldiers, smaller than Americans in size, had been trained to offset this disadvantage by learning judo. Soon after war began in the Pacific, stories filtered back home that burly American soldiers were being dispatched by pint-sized enemies. These reports were not entirely exaggerated, and they underlined the need to train our fighting men in the art of hand-to-hand combat.

Since then, every man who has ever gone through basic training or boot camp has learned the not-so-gentle art of killing an enemy with bare hands. And most every military camp boasted of an instructor who, completely unarmed, would invite anyone in the company to attack him with a knife. Very few recruits made the foolish choice to accept the challenge.

The fundamental principle of ju-jitsu is to use the strength of your opponent as a weapon against himself. This is accomplished by mastering the principles of balance and body leverage. When a small person hurls a husky rival over his or her shoulder, for example, it is the opponent who supplies the momentum. The defender merely supplies the proper leverage.

Oriental self-defense systems go beyond the physical. They involve religious contemplation and spiritual training. The body is brought under the control of the mind. Because of this, a follower is even able to block pain and fear from the conscious mind. No matter what the attack, the objective mind remains unimpaired. For this reason a judo expert is almost unconquerable.

If you enroll in a ju-jitsu class you will wear a loose-fitting pajama-like outfit, and you will learn the Oriental rituals of bowing to your opponent and the like. You will spend many hours working on the mats. First it will be exercising, then learning how to fall, and finally learning the arts of balance and simulated combat.

From watching television you may have gotten the idea that judo experts are sinister villains who lurk in shadows waiting for victims. Quite the opposite is true. Judo is not an attack system. The concentration is on defense. There is hardly any punching or kicking. This doesn't mean that judo is sterile. Any judo throw can cause a lot of damage.

Karate is more violent than ju-jitsu. Students learn fighting stances from which they can lash out with hands, elbows, and feet. The hands are used to deliver fist punches, karate chops, and hand point jabs. However, in exhibitions the punches are always pulled.

If you want to do well in karate you must be nimble in both body and mind. Some of the movements are as intricate as dancing. It is no simple exercise, for example, to unleash a kick while in the middle of a leap. Just try it, if you have any doubts.

Your early classes in a karate school concentrate on exercises designed to put your body in tune. Next, you will be schooled in the art of balance, and you will learn the various blocking stances. You will spend hours practicing fist punches, palm-heel punches, and elbow strikes. As you become an expert you will practice *katas*, dance-like precision routines that simulate combat with one or more opponents. Katas, in a way, are the Oriental equivalent of shadow-boxing.

As with all the martial arts, students of judo and karate are ranked by the color of the belt that they wear over their combat dress. The beginner wears a white belt. As skill develops the belt changes color until the final step is reached, the black belt. The black belt is the sign of the expert, and everything below it is considered to be a student grade.

Success in judo or karate requires a great amount of dedication and more time than the average person is prepared to sacrifice. It is unfortunate that some fly-by-night schools offer quickie self-defense courses. A partial understanding of the martial arts is more dangerous than no knowledge at all, because it gives you a false sense of security. If you decide to enlist in a school, search carefully to find one that has an established reputation for competence and integrity.